ON AN AVERAGE DAY ...
IN THE SOVIET UNION

ALSO BY TOM HEYMANN
Published by Fawcett Columbine

On an Average Day ...

ON AN AVERAGE DAY...

IN THE SOVIET UNION...

TOM HEYMANN

FAWCETT COLUMBINE • NEW YORK

A Fawcett Columbine Book
Published by Ballantine Books

Copyright © 1990 by Thomas N. Heymann

All rights reserved under International and Pan-American Copyright
Conventions. Published in the United States by Ballantine Books, a
division of Random House, Inc., New York, and simultaneously in
Canada by Random House of Canada Limited, Toronto.

Library of Congress Catalog Card Number: 89-92594
ISBN: 0-449-90492-X

Cover design by Dale Fiorillo
Text design by Beth Tondreau Design/Jane Treuhaft

Manufactured in the United States of America

First Edition: September 1990
10 9 8 7 6 5 4 3 2 1

To my son, Gabriel,
whose bright-eyed curiosity
is my continuing inspiration.

ACKNOWLEDGMENTS

I want to thank my friends Lisa Daro and Laurie Lathem for their research assistance and, most importantly, their enthusiasm. I also want to thank Kate Schecter, Sergei Pershman, and Dr. Murray Feshbach for their intelligence and dedication. Also, to my friend, and literary agent, Herbert Katz, who continues to provide invaluable guidance and support. Finally, to my wife, Grace, for her love and objectivity.

AUTHOR'S NOTE

In creating this book, every effort has been made to find the most current data from the most reliable sources available. Interestingly, much of the most reliable information concerning the Soviet Union is generated by professors, research institutes, and government agencies in the United States. The creation of this book, however, owes a great deal to the Soviet government's policy of glasnost. The Soviet Union has always collected a wide range of statistics. It has not, however, until recently, made these figures public.

Much of the information contained in this book was found in newly released Soviet yearbooks, periodicals, and government reports and had to be translated into English by my assistant, Sergei Pershman. Another much used source was the U.S. government's Foreign Broadcast Information Service (FBIS) which covers in great detail the broadcast media of many foreign countries. The United Nations and its health (WHO) and education (UNESCO) divisions also provided a range of interesting information.

Much of today's best original research on the Soviet Union is being collected by Dr. Murray Feshbach of Georgetown University. Dr. Feshbach actually joined the Soviet census-takers in their collection of data for that country's 1989 census. Other important sources included: Radio Liberty, Worldwatch and various trade, professional and public interest groups.

As with any data expressed in terms of averages,

the statistics in this book are often based on estimates, ranges of values, and varying periods of time. In the case of conflicting information from various sources, an attempt was made to weigh the data according to the relative credibility of the sources.

Author's notes have been added to provide additional insight through comparisons and contrasts with the United States. Given the enormous difficulty in obtaining certain specific Soviet information, the notes do not always provide exactly parallel data. Notes do not appear if either the page is self-explanatory or no relevant comparative information could be found.

All monetary statistics are translated at the current official exchange rate of $1.60 per Russian ruble.

INTRODUCTION

Drawing a statistical portrait of the Soviet Union is a task similar to that of photographing a moving object. You must move with your subject or a blurred image will result. As with any statement or observation concerning the Soviet Union, this book must be viewed as a "work in progress," one that presents an ever-changing subject and, consequently, must also be ever-changing.

While many of the statistics contained in this book present a rather grim view of the Soviet Union, there is also cause for optimism. For example, it is only the country's new spirit of glasnost (openness) that allows many of these statistics to be presented, some of them here for the very first time. Also, the country's policy of perestroika (restructuring) is making it easier to trade information, products, and culture. Hopefully, as a result of this trend, we will also be able to increase our exchange of goodwill.

Without question, the Soviet Union has a long way to go to achieve the openness, quality of life, and freedoms that we enjoy, and often take for granted, in the West. Gone, however, is much of the Cold War rhetoric of the past; replaced with hopeful talk of arms reduction, joint space exploration and a cleaner, safer environment.

The Soviet Union is a country of 286,700,000 people (and growing at the rate of 6,658 persons each day). Just slightly larger than the United States (allowing for some interesting comparisons and contrasts), the Soviet Union appears to be on the brink of many revolutionary changes. Here is a look at how our Soviet neighbors live their lives . . . on an average day.

ON AN AVERAGE DAY . . .
IN THE SOVIET UNION

ON AN AVERAGE DAY...

... 15,340 new Soviets are born

... 7,684 Soviets die

In the United States, 10,501 new Americans are born and 5,937 Americans die.

ON AN AVERAGE DAY...

... 1,151 babies are delivered by
midwives, friends, or family members

 In the United States, 384 babies are delivered by midwives,
friends, or family members.

ON AN AVERAGE DAY...

... 122 sets of twins are born

... 1 set of triplets is born

 In the United States, 217 sets of twins and 5 sets of triplets are born.

ON AN AVERAGE DAY...

... the population of the Soviet Union grows by 6,658 persons

Of these,

... 3,617 are men

... 3,041 are women

 In the United States, the population grows by 6,315 persons. Of those, 3,195 are men and 3,120 are women.

ON AN AVERAGE DAY...

... **2,466 Soviets** move from the country to cities

... **41 Soviets** move from cities to the country

 In the United States, 7,359 Americans move from nonmetropolitan areas (country) to metropolitan areas (cities) and 4,805 Americans move from cities to the country.

ON AN AVERAGE DAY...

... the urban population grows by 6,904 persons

... the rural population decreases by 247 persons

In the United States, the urban population grows by 4,962 persons and the rural population grows by 529 persons.

ON AN AVERAGE DAY...

... 6,153 Soviets become teenagers

... 5,633 Soviets turn 18

... 5,096 Soviets turn 40

... 2,055 Soviets turn 65

 In the United States, 8,838 Americans become teenagers, 9,951 Americans turn 18, 10,951 Americans turn 40, and 6,000 Americans turn 65.

☭ON AN AVERAGE DAY...

... 785,526 Russians celebrate birthdays

 In the United States, 673,693 Americans celebrate birthdays.

☭ ON AN AVERAGE DAY...

... 7,698 couples are married
... 2,671 couples are divorced

 In the United States, 6,567 couples are married and 3,197 couples are divorced.

ON AN AVERAGE DAY...

... 1,870 divorces are initiated by women

... 801 are initiated by men

 In the United States, 1,966 divorces are initiated by women, 1,042 are initiated by men, and 189 are initiated jointly.

ON AN AVERAGE DAY...

... 1,336 divorces are blamed on drinking

... 1,233 divorces are blamed on sexual disagreements

In the United States, the leading causes of divorce are: communication problems, basic unhappiness, incompatibility, emotional abuse, financial problems, and sexual problems.

☭ON AN AVERAGE DAY…

… 1,918 children find themselves in a one-parent family because of divorce.

 In the United States, 2,989 children find themselves in a one-parent family because of divorce.

ON AN AVERAGE DAY...

... 1,925 pregnant women get married

... 1,503 babies are born to unmarried women

 In the United States, an estimated 935 pregnant women get married and 2,556 babies are born to unmarried women.

ON AN AVERAGE DAY...

... 3,354 girls under the age of 20 become pregnant

Of those,

... 2,121 receive abortions

... 1,233 give birth

 In the United States, 2,064 girls under the age of 20 become pregnant. Of those, 769 receive abortions and 1,295 give birth.

ON AN AVERAGE DAY...

... 532 children are orphaned or
abandoned

While no reliable numbers on newly orphaned children exist
for the United States, a recent survey estimates that 348 children are abandoned each day. We also know that more than
100,000 children are homeless on any given night.

ON AN AVERAGE DAY...

... there are 973,000 orphans and abandoned children in the Soviet Union

 There are an estimated 900,000 orphans and abandoned children in the United States.

ON AN AVERAGE DAY...

... 104 nationalities are represented in the Soviet Union

Of those,

... 22 have populations of 1,000,000 or more

 In the United States, 21 nationalities have a population of more than one million. Some of the largest ancestry groups include those of English descent (49,596,000), German (49,224,000), Irish (40,166,000), Afro-American (20,965,000), French (12,892,000), Italian (12,184,000), Scottish (10,049,000), Polish (8,228,000), Mexican (7,693,000), and American Indian (6,716,000).

ON AN AVERAGE DAY...

...539 marriages are between couples of
different nationalities

In the United States, there are approximately 799,000 interra-
cial married couples. Nationality statistics are not available.

20

ON AN AVERAGE DAY...

... 29,384 abortions are performed
Of those,
... 17,808 are performed in hospitals

 In the United States, 3,477 abortions are performed. Of those, 3,129 are performed in clinics and doctors' offices. Fewer than 348 are performed in hospitals.

21

☭ON AN AVERAGE DAY...

... 7 mothers die in childbirth

 In the United States, 1 mother dies in childbirth.

ON AN AVERAGE DAY...

... 239 Soviets are reported missing

Of those,

... 191 are found

According to the Federal Bureau of Investigation, there are
68,959 Americans actively categorized as missing.

ON AN AVERAGE DAY...

... 137 children run away from home

 In the United States, 2,740 children run away from home.

ON AN AVERAGE DAY...

... 19 people immigrate to the Soviet Union

... 499 Soviets emigrate to other countries

 1,648 persons immigrate to the United States. An estimated 438 persons emigrate from the United States.

☭ON AN AVERAGE DAY...

... there are 2,000,000 drug abusers in the
Soviet Union

 There are an estimated 9,500,000 drug abusers in the United
States.

ON AN AVERAGE DAY...

... Soviets spend $1,859,693 on illegal drugs

 In the United States, Americans spend $301,369,863 on illegal drugs.

ON AN AVERAGE DAY...

... 807 pounds of heroin are brought into the Soviet Union

Of that,

... 121 pounds are confiscated

 23 pounds of heroin are brought into the United States. Of that, 2.3 pounds are confiscated.

ON AN AVERAGE DAY...

... there are an estimated 21,000,000 alcoholics in the Soviet Union

Of those,

... 18,165,000 are men

... 2,835,000 are women

 In the United States, there are an estimated 10,500,000 alcoholics. Of those, 6,930,000 are men and 3,570,000 are women.

☭ ON AN AVERAGE DAY...

... 17,808 Soviets are arrested for public drunkenness

 2,243 Americans are arrested for public drunkenness.

ON AN AVERAGE DAY...

... 1,170 Soviets are arrested for producing liquor in their homes

From whom the police confiscate,

... 890 home stills

... 11,573 quarts of home-brewed liquor

With liquor readily available in the United States, there is a lessening concern among law enforcement agencies about home brewing. The Bureau of Alcohol, Tobacco and Firearms reports that approximately 6 quarts of home-brewed liquor are confiscated.

ON AN AVERAGE DAY...

...137 Soviets die from alcohol poisoning

 In the United States, 1 American dies from alcohol poisoning. The Soviet Union's unusually high rate is related to the country's large intake of home-processed spirits.

ON AN AVERAGE DAY...

... 674 traffic accidents are reported
   In which,
... 814 Soviets are seriously injured
... 110 Soviets are killed

In the United States, 52,877 traffic accidents are reported in which 3,526 Americans are seriously injured and 120 Americans are killed.

ON AN AVERAGE DAY...

... 2 railroad crossing accidents
   result in,
... 3 injuries
... 1 death

 In the United States, 16 railroad crossing accidents result in 8 injuries and 2 deaths.

ON AN AVERAGE DAY...

... 70,000,000 Soviets smoke

In the United States, 55,000,000 Americans smoke.

ON AN AVERAGE DAY...

... Soviets smoke 203,775,343 cigarettes

 In the United States, Americans smoke 1,562,739,726 cigarettes daily.

☭ON AN AVERAGE DAY...

... 244 Soviets die of lung cancer

 In the United States, 381 Americans die of lung cancer.

ON AN AVERAGE DAY...

... 4,174 Soviets die of heart disease

... 1,245 Soviets die of cancer

... 781 Soviets die in accidents

... 167 Soviets die of pneumonia

... 162 Soviets die of infectious parasitic diseases

... 151 Soviets die in suicides

... 62 Soviets die of tuberculosis

... 18 Soviets die of septicemia

... 15 Soviets die of rheumatic fever

... 12 Soviets die of epilepsy

 In the United States, 2,113 Americans die of heart disease, 1,307 die of cancer, 419 die from strokes, 256 die in accidents, 205 die from chronic obstructive pulmonary disease, 185 die of pneumonia, 101 die of diabetes, 81 die in suicides, and 73 die from liver disease.

CON AN AVERAGE DAY...

... 50 percent of Soviets are seriously
overweight

 In the United States, 25 percent of Americans are seriously
overweight.

ON AN AVERAGE DAY...

... 235 Soviets die of heart attacks
Of those,
... 140 are men
... 95 are women

 In the United States, 1,482 Americans die of heart attacks. Of those, 820 are men and 662 are women.

ON AN AVERAGE DAY...

... 781 Soviets die in accidents
Of those,
... 547 die in alcohol-related accidents

In the United States, 256 Americans die in accidents. Of those,
at least 112 die in alcohol-related accidents.

41

ON AN AVERAGE DAY...

... 41,096 children are hospitalized
Of those,
... 96 are hospitalized due to accidents

In the United States, 7,625 children are hospitalized. Of those, 523 are treated for playground injuries, 359 for toy-related injuries and 236 for injuries associated with nursery equipment. Accidents are the leading cause of death for children.

ON AN AVERAGE DAY...

... 29,400,000 Soviet children cannot swim

The Soviet Union has just 2,500 swimming pools while the United States has approximately 3 million.

☭ON AN AVERAGE DAY...

...55 Soviets drown

Of those,

...17 are children under the age of 15

 In the United States, 14 Americans drown. Of those, 4 are children under the age of 15.

ON AN AVERAGE DAY...

... 247 Soviets are poisoned

Of those,

... 101 die

Of those,

... 7 are children under the age of 15

In the United States, 5,479 Americans are poisoned. Of those, 17 die. Of those, 1 is a child under the age of 15.

ON AN AVERAGE DAY...

... 219 children are born with serious birth defects

... 71 Soviets die from birth-related defects

 In the United States, an estimated 1,638 children are born with serious birth defects. 122 Americans die from birth-related defects.

ON AN AVERAGE DAY...

... 589 children under the age of 14 die

Of those,

... 389 die before reaching their first birthday

In the United States, 78 children under the age of 14 die. Of those, 56 die before reaching their first birthday.

ON AN AVERAGE DAY...

... 3 cases of diphtheria are reported

... 35 cases of typhoid are reported

... 43 cases of syphilis are reported

... 55 cases of whooping cough are reported

... 666 cases of gonorrhea are reported

... 747 cases of measles are reported

... 904 cases of scarlet fever are reported

... 2,359 cases of viral hepatitis are reported

In the United States, 1 case of typhoid is reported, 8 cases of whooping cough, 10 cases of measles, 35 cases of mumps, 157 cases of viral hepatitis, 238 cases of syphilis, 584 cases of chicken pox, and 2,140 cases of gonorrhea.

ON AN AVERAGE DAY...

... 1,707 cases of cancer are diagnosed
   Of those,
... 14 are in children

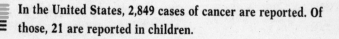

In the United States, 2,849 cases of cancer are reported. Of those, 21 are reported in children.

CON AN AVERAGE DAY...

... 1,245 Soviets die of cancer
   Of those,
... 16 are children

 In the United States, 1,307 Americans die of cancer. Of those, 8 are children.

ON AN AVERAGE DAY...

... 15,000,000 Soviets suffer from
psychiatric illness

 In the United States, an estimated 40,000,000 Americans suffer from mental illness.

ON AN AVERAGE DAY...

... 1,130 Soviets attempt suicide

Of those,

... 525 are men

... 605 are women

In the United States, an estimated 1,181 Americans attempt suicide. Of those, approximately 931 are men and 250 are women.

ON AN AVERAGE DAY...

... 151 Soviets commit suicide

Of those,

... 113 are men

... 38 are women

 In the United States, 84 Americans commit suicide. Of those, 67 are men and 17 are women.

C ON AN AVERAGE DAY...

... 7 children under the age of 20 commit suicide

 In the United States, 7 children under the age of 20 commit suicide.

ON AN AVERAGE DAY...

... the Moscow Suicide Prevention Center receives 80 calls on its adolescent "telephone of trust."

 California's Teen Line receives approximately 46 calls from troubled youths.

ＣON AN AVERAGE DAY...

... less than 15 percent of the Soviet
population uses contraceptives

 According to the National Academy of Sciences, about 95 percent of America's sexually active women of reproductive age
have used contraceptives. Sterilization is the most popular
method, followed by birth control pills, condoms, and dia-
phragms. Still, an estimated 3,288 to 8,219 accidental preg-
nancies occur each day as a result of contraceptive failure.

ON AN AVERAGE DAY...

... the Soviet Union produces 602,740 condoms

... the Soviet Union has an unsatisfied demand for 2,410,959 condoms

In the United States, 1,109,589 condoms are sold. Of those, 443,836 are sold to women.

ON AN AVERAGE DAY...

... approximately 10,000 Soviets carry the AIDS virus

 In the United States, it is estimated that more than 1 million Americans carry the AIDS virus.

ON AN AVERAGE DAY...

... 10 new AIDS cases are reported
Of those,

... 4 are caused by the transfusion of
infected blood during surgery

In the United States, 97 new AIDS cases are reported. Of those, 2 are caused by the transfusion of infected blood.

ON AN AVERAGE DAY...

... the Soviet Union needs 8,219,178 syringes

... the Soviet government delivers 134,247 syringes

Of those,

... 78,082 are delivered without needles

ON AN AVERAGE DAY...

... one 650-bed hospital in Leningrad
receives a daily ration of 1 needle

ON AN AVERAGE DAY...

... there are approximately 1,170,000 doctors in the Soviet Union

Of those,

... 60,000 are obstetric gynecologists

... Of those,

... 30,000 perform abortions exclusively

 In the United States, there are approximately 570,000 doctors. Of those, 31,000 are obstetric gynecologists. Of those, 8,600 perform abortions and, of those, 5,700 perform abortions very rarely.

☭ ON AN AVERAGE DAY...

... 8,680,548 Soviets visit the doctor

Of those,

... 6,423,606 pay bribes to receive better care

 In the United States, 3,482,192 Americans visit the doctor.

ON AN AVERAGE DAY...

... 190,685 Soviets are admitted to hospitals

Of those,

... 141,107 pay bribes to receive better care

 In the United States, 96,438 Americans are admitted to hospitals.

ON AN AVERAGE DAY...

... there are 18,000 hospitals in rural parts of the Soviet Union

Of those,

... 11,700 do not have hot water

... 4,860 do not have sewage systems

... 3,060 do not have running water

There are 6,780 hospitals in the United States. Of those, approximately 3,112 are located in rural parts of the country.

☭ON AN AVERAGE DAY...

...the Ministry of Health receives 181 complaints regarding medical care

 In the United States, state medical boards take disciplinary action against 7 doctors. Of those, 2 are put on probation, 1 has his or her license suspended and 2 have their licenses revoked.

ON AN AVERAGE DAY...

... 7,000,000 Soviets suffer from hearing loss

Of those,

... 1,000,000 are children

In the United States, 20,732,000 Americans suffer from hearing loss. Of those, 1,272,330 are children.

ON AN AVERAGE DAY...

... Moscow has just one shop that
specializes in hearing aids

 New York City has more than 60 shops that specialize in
hearing aids.

ON AN AVERAGE DAY...

... 7,000,000 Soviet children are
physically and mentally handicapped

In the United States, nearly 4,374,000 children are receiving
special education in the schools.

ℭON AN AVERAGE DAY...

... 7,000,000 Soviets suffer from speech defects

 In the United States, an estimated 8,375,000 Americans suffer from speech defects.

ON AN AVERAGE DAY...

... 3,000,000 Soviets suffer from diabetes

Of those,

... 675,000 cannot get adequate
medication

In the United States, 11,000,000 Americans suffer from diabetes. While it is not known exactly how many diabetics cannot obtain adequate medication, many commercial insurance providers routinely refuse to offer nongroup health insurance to people with diabetes.

ON AN AVERAGE DAY...

... 7,000,000 couples suffer from infertility

... $43,835,616 is spent on the treatment of infertility

 In the United States, an estimated 2,400,000 couples suffer from infertility. $2,739,726 is spent on the treatment of infertility.

ON AN AVERAGE DAY...

... 86,805 Soviets visit private (for-profit) medical clinics

... visitors to private medical clinics pay an average of $18.18 for their care

3,482,192 Americans visit private and public medical physicians. First time patients pay an average of $63.51 for the visit and established patients pay $33.91.

ON AN AVERAGE DAY...

... a government-provided abortion costs $8.00

... a nose job at the Moscow Cosmetological Clinic costs $50.00

... a facelift costs $60.00

In the United States, an abortion costs approximately $225. Nose jobs cost an average of $3,750 and a facelift costs an average of $6,000.

ON AN AVERAGE DAY…

… men spend 13 minutes on childcare
… women spend 38 minutes

 In the United States, men spend an average of 7 minutes on childcare while women spend 27 minutes.

☭ON AN AVERAGE DAY...

... men spend 23 minutes preparing meals

... women spend 1 hour and 10 minutes

 In the United States, men spend an average of 15 minutes preparing meals while women spend 51 minutes.

ON AN AVERAGE DAY...

... men spend 13 minutes cleaning house
... women spend 39 minutes

In the United States, men spend an average of 26 minutes
cleaning house while women spend 59 minutes.

ON AN AVERAGE DAY...

... men spend 15 minutes shopping

... women spend 26 minutes

 In the United States, men spend an average of 20 minutes shopping while women spend 38 minutes.

ON AN AVERAGE DAY...

... men spend 3 minutes doing laundry
... women spend 33 minutes

In the United States, men spend an average of 5 minutes doing laundry while women spend 13 minutes.

ON AN AVERAGE DAY...

An average Soviet spends ...

... 43 minutes reading

... 1 hour and 49 minutes watching television

... 5 hours and 7 minutes working

... 7 hours and 50 minutes sleeping

In the United States, Americans spend an average of 27 minutes reading, 2 hours and 29 minutes watching television, 3 hours and 59 minutes working, and 7 hours and 42 minutes sleeping.

ON AN AVERAGE DAY...

... Soviet men spend 20,907,836 hours
waiting on lines to buy alcohol

ON AN AVERAGE DAY...

... an average Soviet spends one and one half hours waiting on lines for food and other essential products

 In the United States, Americans spend an average of 25 minutes waiting on lines.

ON AN AVERAGE DAY...

... the average Soviet earns $11.41
Of that,

... $3.77 is spent on food

... $1.71 is spent on clothing

... $1.69 is spent on education and medical care

... $.92 is spent on taxes

... $.91 is spent on furniture and transportation

... $.83 is put into savings

... $.29 is spent on housing

... $.25 is spent on alcoholic beverages

In the United States, the average American earns $26.83. Of that, $6.15 is spent on furniture and transportation, $5.93 is spent on housing, $5.17 is spent on food, $2.41 is spent on taxes, $1.53 is spent on education and health care, $1.42 is spent on clothing, $1.03 is put into savings and $.29 is spent on alcoholic beverages.

☭ ON AN AVERAGE DAY...

... raising a child costs the average Soviet
family $5.12

 In the United States, raising a child costs the average American family $13.56

ON AN AVERAGE DAY...

An average Soviet consumes ...

... 34 ounces of milk and dairy products

... 13 ounces of bread products

... 10 ounces of vegetables

... 9 ounces of potatoes

... 6 ounces of meat

... 5 ounces of fruit

... 4 ounces of sugar

... 2 ounces of fish

 In the Unites States, the average American consumes 26 ounces of milk and dairy products, 14 ounces of vegetables, 10 ounces of meat, 8 ounces of bread products, 5 ounces of fruit, 3 ounces of potatoes, 3 ounces of sugar, and 1 ounce of fish.

ON AN AVERAGE DAY...

Soviets consume ...

... 3,594,017 gallons of beer

... 1,382,312 gallons of wine

... 1,130,169 gallons of vodka

... 149,721 gallons of champagne

Americans consume: 23,184,658 gallons of beer, 2,291,507 gallons of wine, 223,752 gallons of vodka and 6,585 gallons of champagne.

ON AN AVERAGE DAY...

... Soviets make 4,657,534 long-distance phone calls

Of those,

... 1,164,384 result in wrong numbers due to equipment failures

 Americans make 141,764,398 long-distance phone calls.

ON AN AVERAGE DAY...

... Soviets make 13,602 international phone calls

Of those,

... 1,663 are to Bulgaria

... 1,605 are to Poland

... 1,213 are to Hungary

... 1,162 are to Czechoslovakia

... 1,045 are to East Germany

... 831 are to Yugoslavia

... 825 are to Finland

... 692 are to Italy

... 635 are to West Germany

... 511 are to Mongolia

Americans make 997,466 international phone calls. The most frequently called countries are, in order of frequency: Canada, Mexico, the United Kingdom, West Germany, Japan, France, Italy, Korea, Taiwan, and the Dominican Republic.

ON AN AVERAGE DAY...

... Soviets receive 169,863,014 items through the mail

Of those,

... 638,356 are packages

... 24,109,589 are letters

... 130,958,904 are newspapers and magazines

Americans receive 438,356,164 items through the mail. Of those, approximately 1,778,082 are packages, 28,624,658 are newspapers and magazines, and 225,523,288 are letters.

ON AN AVERAGE DAY...

... Soviets receive 10,032 letters from the United States

... Soviets send 42,451 letters to the United States

ON AN AVERAGE DAY...

... Soviets send 1,482,223 telegrams
   Of those,
... 2,470 are sent to other countries

In the United States, Americans send 52,916 telegrams. Of those, 6,160 are sent to other countries.

ON AN AVERAGE DAY...

... Soviet television broadcasts 149 hours of television programming over 14 channels

... 90 percent of Soviet families can receive just 2 television channels

There are 1,342 television stations and 10,172 cable systems operating in the United States. Many of these broadcast 24 hours per day. The average American home can receive more than 30 channels.

ON AN AVERAGE DAY...

... Soviet radio stations broadcast 235 hours of programming over 14 frequencies

... Radio Moscow broadcasts 300 hours of programming in 77 languages to 100 million foreign listeners.

 There are 4,902 AM and 4,041 FM radio stations in the United States. Many of these broadcast 24 hours per day. The U.S. government's Voice of America (VOA) and government-financed Radio Free Europe and Radio Liberty/Radio Free Afghanistan broadcast 322 hours of programming in 50 languages to approximately 53,500,000 foreign listeners.

ON AN AVERAGE DAY...

... the television broadcast day lasts approximately 13 hours

Of that, approximately

... 5 hours is devoted to news and public affairs

... 4 hours is devoted to films

... 2 hours is devoted to culture/pop culture

... 1 hour is devoted to children's programming

... 30 minutes is devoted to sports

... 30 minutes is devoted to science and travel

In the United States, the broadcast day lasts 24 hours. Of that, approximately 11 hours is devoted to films and entertainment, 9 hours is devoted to news and public affairs, 2 hours is devoted to children's programming and 2 hours is devoted to sports.

ꞏON AN AVERAGE DAY...

... over 10,000 video titles are in circulation

Of those,

... 608 are in the approved government video catalogue

 In the United States, there are more than 40,000 video titles in circulation.

ON AN AVERAGE DAY...

... 4,954 different magazines are available

 There are 11,092 different magazines published in the United States.

C ON AN AVERAGE DAY...

... 8,373 newspapers are published

 There are more than 10,000 newspapers published in the United States.

ON AN AVERAGE DAY...

... daily newspapers have a total circulation of 129,304,000

Of those,

... *Trud* sells 18,700,000

... *Komsomolskaya Pravda* sells 17,600,000

... *Izvestia* sells 10,430,000

In the United States, daily newspapers have a circulation of 63,000,000. Of those, *The Wall Street Journal* has a circulation of 1,869,950, *USA Today* has 1,338,734, *The New York Daily News* has 1,281,706, *The Los Angeles Times* has 1,116,334, and *The New York Times* has 1,038,829.

ON AN AVERAGE DAY...

... *Pravda* receives 1,370 letters to the editor

Of those,

... 16 are printed in the newspaper

The New York Times receives 400 letters to the editor. Of those, 16 are printed in the newspaper.

☭ON AN AVERAGE DAY...

... a full-page advertisement in the
newspaper *Izvestia* costs $50,000

 A full-page advertisement in *The New York Times* costs
$41,000.

ON AN AVERAGE DAY...

Soyuztorgreklama (the Soviet Union's largest advertising agency) ...

... places 82 newspaper ads

... produces 4 television commercials

... produces 3 radio commercials

... prints 646,575 leaflets

Advertising is still in its infancy in the Soviet Union. Advertisers in the United States, meanwhile, spend more than $323,287,671. Of that, $84,931,507 is spent on newspapers, $71,232,877 is spent on television, $57,534,247 is spent on direct mail, $21,917,808 is spent on radio, and $16,438,356 is spent on magazines.

ON AN AVERAGE DAY...

... Russian-language newspapers have a total circulation of 144 million copies

... newspapers in other languages have a total circulation of 40 million copies

 American daily, Sunday, and weekly newspapers have a total circulation of 177,000,000 copies.

CON AN AVERAGE DAY...

... 50 copies of *Time* magazine are sold

... 250 copies of *USA Today* are sold

 In the United States, 624,714 copies of *Time* magazine and 1,338,734 copies of *USA Today* are sold. Approximately 50 copies of the Soviet monthly *Sputnik* are sold in the U.S.

ON AN AVERAGE DAY...

... the average Soviet family subscribes to
6 newspapers and magazines

Approximately 60 percent of American adults read a newspaper. The average American family subscribes to 3 magazines.

ON AN AVERAGE DAY...

... 60,000,000 children watch educational television

... 150,000,000 Soviets watch the evening news program "Vremya"

... 200,000,000 Soviets watch live coverage of the Soviet Congress

In the United States, 38,400,000 Americans watch "The Cosby Show," 37,700,000 watch "Cheers," 33,900,000 watch "A Different World," and 32,500,000 watch "60 Minutes." On an average day, 49,000,000 Americans watch a network evening news broadcast.

ON AN AVERAGE DAY...

... 90 percent of Soviet adults use the nightly television news as their main source of information

 In the United States, 65 percent of Americans use television as their primary source of news.

ON AN AVERAGE DAY...

... 229 new books are published
Of those,

... 7 are general interest

... 8 concern the arts

... 11 are children's books

... 20 concern science

... 32 are literature

... 61 concern the social sciences

... 84 concern the applied sciences

In the United States, 124 new books are published. The most popular subjects include; art (4), literature (5), general interest (6), religion (6), science (8), medicine (9), children's (10), fiction (15), and sociology and economics (22).

ON AN AVERAGE DAY...

... 20 books are translated into Russian
   Of those,

... 2 are translated from English

... 1 is translated from French

... 1 is translated from German

 In the United States, 4 books are translated into English. Of those, 1 is translated from German and 1 is translated from French. The other 2 are translated from assorted languages including: Russian, Italian, Spanish, and Japanese.

ON AN AVERAGE DAY...

... 12 books are published in foreign languages

Of those,

... 3 are published in English

... 1 is published in French

... 1 is published in German

... 1 is published in Spanish

In the United States, 3 books are published in foreign languages.

ℭON AN AVERAGE DAY...

... Soviet libraries receive 383,562 new books

Of those,

... 273,973 will be removed because of a lack of interest

☭ON AN AVERAGE DAY...

... there are 17,000 bookstores in the Soviet Union

... 96 percent of Soviets who buy books have difficulty obtaining their desired title

There are 24,319 bookstores in the United States.

ON AN AVERAGE DAY...

... the Soviet Union has 134,000 libraries

... the Soviet Union has 152,000 movie theaters

 The United States has 116,000 libraries (including public and educational facilities), and 23,000 movie theaters.

ON AN AVERAGE DAY...

... 391,781 Soviets visit libraries
... 11,150,685 Soviets go to the movies

 In the United States, 3,360,827 items are borrowed from public libraries and 2,982,192 Americans attend a movie.

CON AN AVERAGE DAY...

... 477,707 Soviets visit a museum

Of those,

... 100,167 visit art museums

... 218,310 visit archaeology and history
museums

 In the United States, 966,400 Americans visit a museum. Of those, 113,564 visit art museums and 231,474 visit archaeology and history museums.

ON AN AVERAGE DAY...

... 822 theater productions are performed

While most think only of Broadway when they consider the American theater, there are over 200 professional theaters, and countless community theaters, outside of New York City.

# ON AN AVERAGE DAY...

... 326,844 Soviets attend the theater

Of those,

... 35,496 attend musical comedies

... 90,704 attend children's theater

... 200,644 attend dramas

 In the United States, 19,090 persons attend Broadway shows, 44,932 attend operas and musicals (non-Broadway), and 68,767 attend concerts.

ON AN AVERAGE DAY...

... 2,457 Soviets attend the Bolshoi
    Theater

    While there, they consume,

... 3,429 sandwiches

... 11 kilograms of caviar

... 4,000 pastries

... 1,714 cups of coffee

ON AN AVERAGE DAY...

... 11,624 Soviets travel abroad

... 16,438 foreigners visit the Soviet Union

 In the United States, 113,151 Americans travel abroad and 24,274 foreigners visit the U.S.

ON AN AVERAGE DAY...

... 159 Soviets visit the United States

... 231 Americans visit the Soviet Union

ON AN AVERAGE DAY...

... 150,000 Soviet citizens live in foreign countries

 More than 2,000,000 Americans live in foreign countries.

ON AN AVERAGE DAY...

... 200 Soviet students are participating in foreign exchange programs in the United States

... 1,100 American students are participating in foreign exchange programs in the Soviet Union

ON AN AVERAGE DAY...

... 1,444 Soviet college students are studying in foreign countries

Of those,

... 193 are studying in the United States

ON AN AVERAGE DAY...

... 120,000 foreign college students are studying in the Soviet Union

Of those,

... 592 are from the United States

ON AN AVERAGE DAY...

... there are 130,000 schools in the Soviet Union

Of those,

... 65,000 do not have central heating, running water, or sewage facilities

 There are 109,000 schools in the United States. Few, if any, are without basic amenities.

☭ON AN AVERAGE DAY...

... 42,000,000 Soviet children attend
school

 There are more than 45,000,000 schoolchildren in the United
States.

ON AN AVERAGE DAY...

... 127,400 schools teach computer usage
   Of those,
... 2,080 have computers

In the United States, more than 95 percent of schools teach computer usage. All of these schools teach students on actual microcomputers.

ON AN AVERAGE DAY...

... the Soviet Union has more than 27,000,000 phones

... 58,000,000 Soviets are on a waiting list to receive a phone

Of those,

... 1,548 receive phones

The United States has more than 118,000,000 phones—more than any other country in the world.

ON AN AVERAGE DAY...

... Soviets have to apply for 4,320,393 documents

... the combined efforts of issuing and receiving these documents costs $23,013,699

ON AN AVERAGE DAY...

... Soviets waste 4,657,534 hours
obtaining unnecessary papers

... Soviet bureaucrats spend 76,164 hours
issuing these documents

ON AN AVERAGE DAY...

... 156,164,384 Soviets travel on public transportation

Of those,

... 128,767,123 travel by bus

... 13,698,630 travel by subway

Of those,

... 7,500,000 travel on the Moscow Metro

In the United States, 24,293,151 Americans ride on public transportation. Of those, 15,800,000 travel by bus and 6,323,288 travel by subway. Of those, 3,700,000 ride the New York City subway system.

ON AN AVERAGE DAY...

... Aeroflot (the Soviet national airline) carries 342,466 passengers

Of those,

... 11,507 are carried on international flights

 American-owned airlines carry 1,174,940 passengers. Of those, 35,214 are carried on international flights.

ON AN AVERAGE DAY...

... 24 flights are delayed or must land to refuel because of insufficient fuel allocations

... 68,493 passengers are delayed

... delayed passengers are paid $948,443 in compensation

U.S. airlines receive 112 complaints. Of those, 55 are for flight cancellations, delays, or passenger bumping.

ON AN AVERAGE DAY...

... 41,096 passengers are turned away from airports because of insufficient capacity

In the United States, 2,133 passengers are turned away from flights because of insufficient capacity. Of those, 353 are "bumped" involuntarily. The remainder exchange their seats for compensation.

ON AN AVERAGE DAY...

- ... 151 new "cooperatives" (private businesses) begin operation
- ... 7,890 Soviets begin work at cooperative businesses

 In the United States, 1,876 new businesses are incorporated. Private sector employment increases by 6,519 Americans.

ON AN AVERAGE DAY...

... retail trade increases by $90,410,959

Of that,

... $27,123,288 is due to the increased sale of alcohol

... $22,602,740 is due to inflation

In the United States, retail trade increases by $200,273,973. Of that, $7,009,589 is due to inflation while liquor sales decrease by $273,973.

ON AN AVERAGE DAY...

... 217 patents are issued

Of those,

... 4 are issued to foreign registrants

 In the United States, 243 patents are issued. Of those, 114 are issued to foreign registrants.

ON AN AVERAGE DAY...

... Soviets begin 1 new joint venture with foreign companies

ON AN AVERAGE DAY...

... the Soviet Union is engaged in 365 joint ventures with foreign companies

Of those,

... 50 are with companies from Socialist countries

... 315 are with companies from Capitalist countries

Of those,

... 26 are with West Germany

... 14 are with Italy

... 13 are with the United States

... 12 are with Great Britain

... 8 are with France

... 8 are with Japan

... 6 are with Canada

ON AN AVERAGE DAY...

... the Soviet Union exports $1,545,205 worth of goods to the United States

... the Soviet Union imports $7,805,479 worth of goods from the United States

ON AN AVERAGE DAY...

The Soviet Union exports to the United States ...

... 82 pounds of caviar

... 28,356 bottles of Stolichnaya vodka

 Nearly 80 percent of U.S. exports to the Soviet Union are agricultural products, including: 112,314,000 pounds of corn, 32,004,000 pounds of wheat and 1,794,000 pounds of soybeans.

ON AN AVERAGE DAY...

The Soviet Union imports ...

... 821,918 razor blades

... 82,192 pairs of pantyhose

... 41,096 dresses

Some popular U.S. imports include: 12,192 automobiles, 29,492 televisions, and 2,576,438 pairs of shoes.

ON AN AVERAGE DAY...

... approximately 5,000 Visa cards are issued

 In the United States, the number of Visa cards increases by 24,658. The Soviet Union is just beginning its use of credit cards and has fewer than one million in circulation. Americans, by contrast, hold more than 841 million credit cards.

ON AN AVERAGE DAY...

... Soviets drink 2,958,904 bottles of Pepsi
... Soviets eat 1,667 slices of American pizza

 Americans spend $35,616,438 on Pepsi and $54,794,521 on pizza, both long-time favorites in the United States.

ON AN AVERAGE DAY...

... more than 15,000 Soviets eat at the
Moscow McDonald's

 While this number is insignificant in comparison to the more
than 16,000,000 Americans who eat at McDonald's, there are
plans to build at least 20 new McDonald's restaurants in the
Soviet Union in the coming years.

ON AN AVERAGE DAY...

... the country's anti-drinking campaign (including the restricted production and sale of alcoholic beverages) costs the government $42,507,264 in lost tax revenues

In the United States, an estimated $319,726,027 is lost due to alcohol-related losses in productivity. The U.S. also spends an estimated $41,095,890 on alcoholism treatment.

ON AN AVERAGE DAY...

... the government spends $48,219,178 on environmental protection

... the government spends $51,232,877 in interest on its national debt

In the United States, the Federal government spends $13,424,658 on the Environmental Protection Agency (EPA) and $445,205,480 in interest on the national debt.

ON AN AVERAGE DAY...

... the government spends $166,136,986 on education

... the government spends $355,945,206 on defense

 In the United States, the Federal government spends $46,027,400 on education and $807,260,270 on defense.

ON AN AVERAGE DAY...

... the government spends $96,438,356 on healthcare

... the government spends $142,904,110 on weapons and equipment

The United States government spends $136,331,507 on healthcare and $322,394,521 on the research, testing, and procurement of arms and weapons.

ON AN AVERAGE DAY...

... 6,123 Soviets are drafted into the
    military

   Of those,

... 1,378 are not fluent in Russian

... 398 have criminal records

 In the United States, 814 Americans enlist in the armed
forces. Of those, 57 have not graduated from high school.

ON AN AVERAGE DAY...

... the Soviet Union has 160 spy satellites in space

 The United States has between four and five spy satellites in space. These satellites, however, are far more capable than the Soviet instruments.

ON AN AVERAGE DAY...

... the Soviet Union spends $2,191,781 collecting Western technology

... the exploitation of Western technology saves the Soviet military $22,739,726, and,

... costs the United States and its Allies $24,931,507

ON AN AVERAGE DAY...

The Soviet military manufactures ...

... 22 surface-to-air missiles

... 5 tanks

... 2 sea-launched cruise missiles

... 1 jet fighter

... 1 military helicopter

The U.S. Department of Defense manufactures 22 surface-to-air missiles, 2 tanks, 2 sea-launched cruise missiles, 1 jet fighter, and 1 military helicopter.

ON AN AVERAGE DAY...

... the Soviet Union sells $34,246,575 in weapons

Of that ...

... $27,123,288 is sold to Third World countries

The United States sells $25,205,479 in arms. Of that, $9,589,041 is sold to Third World countries.

ON AN AVERAGE DAY...

... 2,424,335 pounds of pesticides are
   applied to crops

Of that,

... 969,734 pounds are applied by air

In the United States, 2,739,726 pounds of pesticides are applied to crops. With the increased use of aircraft application,
however, only 2,740 pounds reach their target.

ON AN AVERAGE DAY...

... 18,975,000 Soviet children suffer from allergies as a result of exposure to pesticides

 At least 3,000,000 American children are exposed to amounts of pesticides exceeding governmentally accepted levels. This exposure will lead to hundreds of additional cancer cases and the increased incidence of neurological and behavioral impairments.

℃ON AN AVERAGE DAY...

... 15,340 babies are born

Of those,

... 1,382 suffer from abnormalities due to alcoholism among their mothers or exposure to pesticides

 Of the 10,501 babies born in the United States, 1,027 are born to mothers who use drugs, including alcohol. While the body of evidence is still quite limited, there appears to be a strong correlation between a mother's exposure to pesticides and the incidence of birth defects.

ON AN AVERAGE DAY...

... 14,520,547,950 gallons of untreated sewage are dumped into Soviet waterways

Of that,

... 821,918 pounds of toxic chemicals are dumped into the Volga River

... water pollution costs the Soviet Union $120,547,945

6,301,369,863 gallons of untreated sewage are dumped into America's waterways. 635,616 pounds of toxic chemicals are dumped into the Mississippi River. Water pollution costs the United States $95,890,411.

ON AN AVERAGE DAY...

... 30,000,000 Soviets drink polluted water

Resulting in,

... 32 cases of typhoid

 In the United States, 117,000,000 Americans drink underground well water. Industry is responsible for the injection of 8,767,123 pounds of toxic substances into underground wells. Of those wells tested, 1 in 9 shows harmful levels of pesticides.

ON AN AVERAGE DAY...

The Soviet Union dumps 350,684,931 pounds of harmful substances into the atmosphere ...

Of that,

... 6,301,370 pounds are chlorofluorocarbons (CFCs), contributing to ozone depletion

... 50,228,310 pounds are carbon dioxide, contributing to global warming

... 153,424,658 pounds are sulfur dioxide, contributing to acid rain

The United States dumps 764,026,849 pounds of harmful substances into the atmosphere. Of that, 7,704,110 pounds are CFCs, 62,182,648 pounds are carbon dioxide, and 128,048,000 pounds are sulfur dioxide.

ꙩ ON AN AVERAGE DAY...

... 50,000,000 Soviets breathe unhealthful air

 More than 100,000,000 Americans breathe unhealthful air.

ON AN AVERAGE DAY...

... 162,868 Soviets become ill with the flu

In the United States, 202,192 Americans become ill with the flu.

ON AN AVERAGE DAY...

... 3,835,616 workdays are lost to illness
Of those,

... approximately 575,342 are caused by mothers' absenteeism due to their children's illnesses

 In the United States, 1,663,014 workdays are lost to illness. Companies lose $10,958,904 due to employee absenteeism related to childcare emergencies.

ON AN AVERAGE DAY...

... 245,000 Soviets miss work because
they are drunk during working hours

Of those,

... 16 are arrested for drinking at work

 Alcohol abuse costs the United States $194,520,548 in lost em-
ployment and reduced productivity.

ON AN AVERAGE DAY...

... 3,500,000 Soviets work in unsafe conditions

... 1,890 Soviets are injured in work-related accidents

... 40 Soviets die in work-related accidents

In the United States, an estimated 8,500,000 Americans work at sites where the noise level alone presents an increased risk of hearing loss. This and other factors cause 521 occupational illnesses. Work-related accidents injure 4,932 Americans and kill 29 more.

ON AN AVERAGE DAY...

... 30,000 Soviets are not at their jobs because of strikes

 In the United States, 12,277 Americans are not at their jobs because of strikes.

ON AN AVERAGE DAY...

... 500,000 workers are diverted from their regular jobs by the government

Of those,

... 212,000 are sent to work in agriculture

... 84,500 are sent to work on construction sites

... 20,000 are sent to work at fruit and vegetable depots

... 5,714 are sent to talent contests and sports competitions

ON AN AVERAGE DAY...

... the Soviet Union produces 25,000,000 different products

Of those,

... 23,000,000 have their retail prices set by the government

☭ON AN AVERAGE DAY...

... 1,100 common consumer items are in short supply

ON AN AVERAGE DAY...

... 2,500,000 "migrant shoppers" travel to
Moscow in search of essential goods

ON AN AVERAGE DAY...

... unsatisfied demand for consumer goods is approximately $144,000,000,000

   Including demand for,

... 1,500,000 televisions

... 275,000,000 pairs of shoes

... 600,000 refrigerators

ON AN AVERAGE DAY...

... the Soviet Union produces 26,301 televisions

Of those,

... 5,155 are rejected as being substandard

ON AN AVERAGE DAY...

... faulty television sets cause 10 fires

... 1 person is killed or injured by televisions

In the United States, faulty televisions are responsible for 30 fires. 84 Americans are injured by televisions.

ON AN AVERAGE DAY...

... the Soviet Union produces 2,246,575 pairs of shoes

Of those,

... 449,315 pairs are rejected as being substandard

ON AN AVERAGE DAY...

... the Soviet Union has an unsatisfied demand for 20,000,000 VCRs

... the Soviet Union produces 192 VCRs

In the United States, Americans purchase 28,219 new VCRs. More than 60 percent of American homes have a VCR.

ON AN AVERAGE DAY...

... the Soviet Union has an unsatisfied demand for 4,000,000 cars

... the Soviet Union produces 3,562 cars

Of those,

... 1,175 are exported

In the United States, 19,449 cars are produced. Of those, 1,734 are exported.

℣ON AN AVERAGE DAY...

... the Soviet Union has 300,000 trained computer operators

... the Soviet Union has 200,000 personal computers

 In the United States, there are 37,750,000 personal computers. There are at least that many trained operators.

ON AN AVERAGE DAY...

... the Soviet Union has an unsatisfied demand for 28,000,000 personal computers

... the Soviet Union produces 274 personal computers

... the Soviet Union imports 151 personal computers

There are nearly 40 million personal computers in the United States. More than 25,000 additional units are sold daily.

ON AN AVERAGE DAY...

... travelers bring 60 personal computers into the Soviet Union

ON AN AVERAGE DAY...

... 240,828,000 Soviets get the goods they need through the black market

... 20,000,000 Soviets earn their living through the black market

In the United States, an estimated 265,000 Americans are employed in the underground economy (black market).

ON AN AVERAGE DAY...

... an IBM-compatible personal computer sells for $54,000

... an IBM-XT compatible personal computer sells for $80,000

... an IBM-AT compatible personal computer sells for $130,000

In the United States, genuine IBM computers sell for $2,000 to $5,000. With the announced opening of Computerland and MicroAge stores in the Soviet Union, however, prices there should begin to fall somewhat. But, higher prices will continue to prevail as only dollars will be accepted as payment.

ON AN AVERAGE DAY...

... a pair of Levi's 501 jeans sell for $400
... a VCR sells for $9,600

In the United States, a pair of Levi jeans sells for approximately $25 and a VCR sells for approximately $350.

ON AN AVERAGE DAY...

... Soviets spend $1,095,890,411 on goods obtained through the black market

... Soviets spend $58,447,489 on services obtained through the black market

 Americans spend an estimated $273,972,603 on goods and services through the underground economy (black market).

ON AN AVERAGE DAY...

... Soviets have $480,000,000,000 in savings banks

... Soviets have $216,000,000,000 outside of Soviet banks (in mattresses, illegal savings accounts, crime underground etc.)

Americans have an estimated $985,500,000,000 in savings accounts, CDs, etc. An additional $243,000,000,000 is circulating outside of U.S. banks. Much of this is thought to be in use in foreign countries as a second currency, and within the U.S. crime underground.

ON AN AVERAGE DAY...

... there are 6,850 millionaires in the Soviet Union

Of those,

... 350 made their fortunes legally

In the United States, there are estimated to be more than one million millionaires. We can only guess how many of those fortunes were made illegally.

ON AN AVERAGE DAY...

... 5,116 crimes are committed

... 3,523 Soviets are arrested

... 1,126 Soviets are sent to prison

 In the United States, 93,474 crimes are committed, 34,474 Americans are arrested and 1,593 Americans are sent to state and federal prisons.

ON AN AVERAGE DAY...

... **504 crimes are committed by minors**

... **830 crimes are committed by ex-convicts**

... **992 crimes are committed by persons under the influence of alcohol**

 Of the 34,826 crimes committed daily in the United States, 4,330 crimes are committed by minors, 21,766 are committed by ex-convicts, and 6,443 are committed by persons under the influence of alcohol.

ON AN AVERAGE DAY...

... **241 Soviets are arrested for drunken driving**

Of those,

... **49 are government officials**

In the United States, 4,932 Americans are arrested for driving under the influence of alcohol.

ON AN AVERAGE DAY...

... drunk driving costs the Soviet Union $13,150,685 in damages

 Drunk driving costs the United States $65,753,425 in damages.

ON AN AVERAGE DAY...

... 166 Soviets are robbed

... 102 Soviets are assaulted

... 46 Soviets are murdered

In the United States, 3,786 Americans are assaulted, 1,704 are robbed, and 49 are murdered.

ON AN AVERAGE DAY...

... 48 rapes and attempted rapes are reported

Of those,

... 16 are committed by minors

 In the United States, 86 rapes are reported. Of those, 13 are committed by minors.

ON AN AVERAGE DAY...

... 482 homes are burglarized

   Resulting in the loss of,

... $54,795 in cash and valuables

In the United States, 11,800 homes are burglarized resulting in the loss of approximately $9,440,000 in cash and valuables.

ON AN AVERAGE DAY...

... 381 fires are reported
Of those,
... 23 are started by arson

 In the United States, 6,675 fires are reported. Of those, 240 are started by arson.

ON AN AVERAGE DAY...

Fires cause ...

... the death of 23 Soviets

... $1,481,644 in damages

In the United States, fires cause the death of 13 Americans and $19,693,151 in damages.

ON AN AVERAGE DAY...

... there are more than 16,000,000 guns in the Soviet Union

... there are 4,300,000 Soviet hunters

 There are an estimated 1,000,000 assault rifles and 60,000,000 handguns in the United States. There are just under 16,000,000 American hunters.

ON AN AVERAGE DAY...

Hunters kill ...

... 227 wild boars

... 268 foxes

... 345 deer

... 3,822 rabbits

In the United States, hunters kill 3 wolves, 61 bears, 685 coyotes, 959 wild turkeys, 12,603 deer, 60,274 squirrels and 68,493 rabbits.

ON AN AVERAGE DAY...

... firearms are used to commit 10 crimes
   Of those,
... 2 are murders
... 1 is armed robbery
... 1 is assault

 In the United States, firearms are used to commit at least 1,400 crimes. Of those, 35 are murders, 255 are armed robberies, and 643 are assaults.

ON AN AVERAGE DAY...

... 132 firearms are confiscated by the police

 608 Americans are arrested for illegal possession of a weapon.

ON AN AVERAGE DAY...

... 2,607 organized criminal groups operate in the Soviet Union

Of those,

... 200 are related to the Mafia

 In the United States, there are approximately 1,700 sworn Mafia members. For each member, there are at least 10 additional associates. The FBI estimates that there are 25 independent Mafia families operating in the U.S.

ON AN AVERAGE DAY...

... 800,000 Soviets are serving prison terms

Of those,

... 219,200 are under the age of 25

... 200,000 are alcoholics or drug addicts

... 92,000 have been convicted of murder

... 8,000 are over the age of 60

In the United States, 556,748 Americans are serving prison terms. Of those, 154,776 are under the age of 25, 237,175 are regular drug or alcohol users, 68,480 have been convicted of murder, and 6,124 are over the age of 60.

☭ON AN AVERAGE DAY...

... 27,587 minors are serving terms in Soviet prisons

Of those,

... 2,759 are orphans

... 1,875 have been in prison before

... 1,324 are girls

... 557 have been convicted of murder

 In the United States, 91,646 minors are serving time in jails and juvenile detention facilities. Of those, 14,755 are orphans, 77,082 have been in prison before, 19,035 are girls and 1,650 have been convicted of murder.

ON AN AVERAGE DAY...

... 1,233 Soviets are released from prison
Of those,

... 90 are homeless because of
government regulations prohibiting
convicts from receiving residence
permits

In the United States, 23,038 Americans are released from
prison.

☭ON AN AVERAGE DAY...

... 1,500,000 Soviets are homeless

 In the United States, between 3,000,000 and 4,000,000 Americans are homeless.

 # ON AN AVERAGE DAY...

... 14 million Soviet families are on waiting lists for improved housing

... 5 million Soviet families are currently living in housing that is dilapidated or hazardous

 In the United States, just 29 percent of eligible households are currently receiving housing assistance. The average wait for government-assisted housing is 21 months. 6,428,000 housing units have moderate or severe physical problems.

ON AN AVERAGE DAY...

... 28,318,650 Soviets share housing with non-relatives

... 6,027 new housing units are constructed

 In the United States, more than 10,500,000 Americans share housing with non-relatives. 3,895 new housing units are constructed.

ON AN AVERAGE DAY...

... 10,700,000 households are comprised
of two or more families

... 1,070,000 do not have running water
from a well or a municipality

 2,638,000 households are comprised of two or more families.
761,000 households do not have running water from a well or
a municipality.

☭ON AN AVERAGE DAY...

... 40,000,000 Soviets live in poverty
Of those,
... 35,000,000 are retired persons

 In the United States, 32,500,000 Americans live in poverty. Of those, 3,500,000 are 65 years or older.

ON AN AVERAGE DAY...

... 4,500,000 Soviets are unemployed

In the United States, an estimated 6,500,000 Americans are
unemployed.

ON AN AVERAGE DAY...

... there are 4,000,000 disabled persons in the Soviet Union

Of those,

... 1,000,000 currently hold jobs

 In the United States, there are 13,420,000 disabled persons. Of those, approximately 8,521,700 have been returned to gainful employment through vocational rehabilitation.

ON AN AVERAGE DAY...

... approximately 6,055,104 Soviets are
homosexuals

Of those,

... 4,036,736 are men

... 2,018,368 are women

In the United States, an estimated 10 percent of the population—11,853,100 men and 12,486,900 women—is homosexual.

ON AN AVERAGE DAY...

... there are approximately 15,000 houses of worship in the Soviet Union

Of those,

... 6,794 are Russian Orthodox

... 2,976 are Evangelical Christian or Baptist

... 1,099 are Catholic

... 843 are Pentecostal

... 751 are Islamic

... 445 are Seventh Day Adventist

... 378 are Jehovah's Witness

... 109 are Jewish

 There are approximately 346,102 houses of worship in the United States. Of those, 315,810 are Catholic, 23,561 are Protestant, 3,416 are Jewish, 1,662 are Eastern religions, and 100 are Buddhist.

ON AN AVERAGE DAY...

... 4 new religious congregations are registered

Of those,

... 3 are Russian Orthodox

While the number of churches in the United States has remained stable, membership is declining at the rate of 347 daily.

ON AN AVERAGE DAY...

... the government returns 3 previously confiscated church buildings to religious groups

ON AN AVERAGE DAY...

... religious groups conduct 5,893 ceremonies

Of those,

... 69 are confirmations

... 219 are weddings

... 2,375 are christenings

... 3,230 are funerals

Overall statistics are not available, but 76 percent of first marriages and 58 percent of remarriages are consumated by religious ceremonies. We also know that Catholic churches in the United States baptize 2,570 Americans, convert 224 Americans to Catholicism, and preside over 936 marriages and 1,242 deaths.

ON AN AVERAGE DAY...

... the Soviet Union prints 1,619 Bibles

... the Soviet Union imports 3,288 Bibles

In the United States, 154,491 Bibles are sold.

ON AN AVERAGE DAY...

... the Soviet Union spends $575,342 on psychic research

According to a CBS News poll, two-thirds of Americans believe in psychic powers and 25 percent have experienced paranormal phenomena.

ON AN AVERAGE DAY...

... 277,000 Soviets are registered boxers

... 500,000 Soviets study the oriental martial arts

... 5,000,000 Soviets play billiards

America's favorite participation sports are: swimming, exercise walking, bicycle riding, basketball, jogging, volleyball, aerobics, softball, golf, and tennis.

ON AN AVERAGE DAY...

... the Soviet Union has 42,000,000 cows

... the Soviet Union has 1,500,000 milkmaids

Of those,

... 1,350,000 do not get enough sleep

There are 10,127,000 milk cows in the United States. Of those, fewer than 50,000 are milked by hand.

CON AN AVERAGE DAY...

... 410,959 Soviets attend the circus

... the Soviet Union has 72 permanent circus buildings

 More than 1,000,000 Americans attend the country's 125 active circuses. There are no permanent circus buildings in the United States. While extremely popular in the Soviet Union, the circus is still considered to be a luxury item; not readily affordable to the average family.

ON AN AVERAGE DAY...

... there are approximately 250,000 rock
groups in the Soviet Union

Americans spend $16,986,301 on prerecorded music. Of that,
$7,847,671 is spent on the "rock" category.

ON AN AVERAGE DAY...

... 247 "classified" statistics are made public by the government

 The U.S. government declassifies 13,499 documents. Of those, 135 were originally classified as "top secret," 4,185 were "secret," and 9,179 were "confidential."

NOTES
AND
INDEX

 **SOURCE**

3. *USSR and the Foreign Countries* (*USSR*)
4. Same
   Dr. Murray Feshbach, Georgetown University
5. Same
6. *Izvestia*
7. Soviet Union
8. *Izvestia*
9. Dr. Murray Feshbach
10. Radio Liberty
11. *USSR*
12. *Time*
13. *Maclean's*
    World Press Review
14. Radio Liberty
15. *Time*
    USSR
    Radio Liberty
16. United Nations
    World Press Review
    USSR's People's Economy for 70 Years (*People's Economy*)
17. Consumer Markets Abroad
    Radio Liberty
18. Same
19. *The New York Times*
20. *Soviet Life*
21. Dr. Murray Feshbach
22. Same
    Izvestia
23. Same
24. *Pravda*

SOURCE

3. *On An Average Day*
4. National Center for Health Statistics
5. *On An Average Day*
6. *Statistical Abstract of the United States*
7. Bureau of the Census
8. *Statistical Abstract*
9. *On An Average Day*
10. Same
11. Same
12. National Center for Health Statistics
13. *Journal of Marriage and the Family*
14. *Statistical Abstract*
15. National Center for Health Statistics
16. Same
17. *The New York Times*
On An Average Day
18. *USA Today*
19. *Statistical Abstract*
20. Same
21. *On An Average Day*
American College of Obstetricians and Gynecologists
22. National Center for Health Statistics
23. FBI
24. *Statistical Abstract*

SOURCE

25. *Moscow News*
    Radio Liberty
    Izvestia
    Foreign Broadcast Information Service (FBIS)
    National Conference on Soviet Jewry
26. Dr. Murray Feshbach
27. FBIS
28. *Current*
    FBIS
29. Radio Liberty
30. *Izvestia*
31. Same
32. *Soviet Geography*
33. *World Press Review*
34. Radio Liberty
35. Dr. Murray Feshbach
36. *Tobacco Reporter*
    USSR
37. Dr. Murray Feshbach
38. World Health Organization (WHO)
    Dr. Murray Feshbach
39. *Time*
40. WHO
41. Same
    Worldwatch
42. *Izvestia*
    Dr. Murray Feshbach
43. FBIS
    Moscow News
44. WHO

25. *On An Average Day*
26. National Center for Health Statistics
27. *USA Today*
28. *On An Average Day*
29. National Council on Alcoholism
30. FBI
31. Bureau of Alcohol, Tobacco and Firearms
32. National Safety Council
33. Same
34. *USA Today*
    National Safety Council
35. *On An Average Day*
36. Same
37. American Lung Association
38. *On An Average Day*
39. *Wall Street Journal*
40. *On An Average Day*
    National Center for Health Statistics
41. *On An Average Day*
    National Council for Alcoholism
42. *Statistical Abstract*
    National Safety Council
    On An Average Day
43. *Moscow News*
44. National Safety Council

SOURCE

45. *Izvestia*
    WHO
46. *Izvestia*
    Dr. Murray Feshbach
47. *Izvestia*
48. Dr. Murray Feshbach
    United States Congress
49. United States Department of Commerce
    Izvestia
50. WHO
    Izvestia
51. Same
52. FBIS
    Radio Liberty
53. Dr. Murray Feshbach
    Radio Liberty
54. Same
    Ogonyok
55. Radio Liberty
56. Same
57. *Maclean's*
58. Dr. Murray Feshbach
59. Same
    Radio Liberty
60. FBIS
61. *U.S. News & World Report*
62. *USSR Facts & Figures Annual*
    Radio Liberty
63. U.S. Congress
    Dr. Murray Feshbach
64. Same

SOURCE

45. Same
46. National Network to Prevent Birth Defects
    National Center for Health Statistics
47. National Center for Health Statistics
48. Centers for Disease Control
49. American Cancer Society
50. National Center for Health Statistics
51. *Psychology Today*
52. American Association of Suicidology
53. National Center for Health Statistics
54. Same
55. Cedars Sinai Medical Center, Los Angeles
56. *The New York Times*
57. *On An Average Day*
58. U.S. Centers for Disease Control (CDC)
59. Same
62. *Statistical Abstract*
    The New York Times
63. *Statistical Abstract*
64. Same

SOURCE

65. *Moscow News*
    U.S. News & World Report
66. U.S. Congress
67. *Newsweek*
68. *Izvestia*
69. *Argumenty I Fakty*
70. *Moscow News*
71. *Izvestia*
    Moscow News
72. *Pravda*
73. *Moscow News*
74. *The New York Times*
    Vogue
75. John P. Robinson, Survey Research Center, University of Maryland
76. Same
77. Same
78. Same
79. Same
80. Same
81. *Izvestia*
82. *Pravda International*
    FBIS
83. *Soviet Review*
84. FBIS
85. United States Department of Agriculture
86. *Soviet Geography*
87. U.S. Congress
    Forbes
88. AT&T

SOURCE

65. American Hospital Association
66. Federation of State Medical Boards
67. *Statistical Abstract*
68. NYNEX *Yellow Pages*
69. Same
70. National Institutes of Health
71. American Diabetes Association
72. American Fertility Society
73. *Statistical Abstract*
    American Medical Association
74. American College of Obstetricians & Gynecologists
    American Association of Plastic and Reconstructive
    Surgeons
75. *On An Average Day*
76. Same
77. Same
78. Same
79. Survey Research Center, University of Maryland
80. Same
82. *On An Average Day*
83. U.S. Department of Labor
84. *The New York Times*
85. *Statistical Abstract*
86. Department of Agriculture
    Business Week
    Champagne News and Information Bureau
87. AT&T
88. Same

SOURCE

89. *USSR*
   Central Statistical Board of the USSR
90. United States Postal Service
91. International Telecommunications Union
92. Radio Liberty
   Pravda
93. *Soviet Life*
   Pravda
94. Ellen Mickiewicz, Emory University
95. Radio Liberty
96. *World Press Review*
97. Same
98. USSR
   Moscow News
99. *Soviet Life*
100. *Adweek's Marketing Week*
101. *Wall Street Journal*
102. *World Press Review*
103. *USA Today*
   FBIS
104. *Soviet Life*
105. Same
   The New York Times
106. U.S. Congress
107. UNESCO
108. Same
109. Same
110. Radio Liberty
111. *The New York Times*
   Radio Liberty

SOURCE

89. U.S. Postal Service
91. International Telecommunications Union (ITU)
92. A.C. Nielsen
93. *Statistical Abstract*
    "Voice of America"
94. Author's Research
95. *Variety*
96. Magazine Publishers of America
97. American Newspaper Publishers Association
98. Same
99. *The New York Times*
100. Same
101. *USA Today*
102. American Newspaper Publishers Association
103. *USA Today*
     Time
     Sputnik
104. American Newspaper Publishers Association
     Magazine Publishers of America
105. *USA Today*
106. *USA Today*
107. *Statistical Abstract*
108. UNESCO
109. *Books in Print*
111. American Book Trade Directory

SOURCE

112. Central Statistical Board of the USSR
113. *Izvestia*
    Central Statistical Board of the USSR
114. UNESCO
115. *The New York Times*
116. UNESCO
117. *Soviet Life*
118. FBIS
    Izvestia
119. FBIS
    WHO
120. FBIS
121. American Council of Teachers in Russia
122. Institute of International Education
123. Same
    Moscow News
124. FBIS
    Phi Delta Kappan
    Moscow News
125. FBIS
    Phi Delta Kappan
126. U.S. Congress
127. *Financial World*
    AT&T
128. *Soviet Life*
129. Same
130. *Izvestia*
    FBIS
    Popular Mechanics
131. *Aviation Week and Space Technology*

SOURCE

112. American Library Association
     The New York Times
113. *On An Average Day*
114. UNESCO
115. *Fortune*
116. *Statistical Abstract*
118. *On An Average Day*
120. *Statistical Abstract*
124. National Center for Education Statistics
125. Same
126. Same
127. AT&T
130. American Public Transportation Association
     New York City Transit Authority
131. *Statistical Abstract*

SOURCE

132. *Izvestia*
     The New York Times
133. *Aviation Week and Space Technology*
134. *Business Week*
     Pravda
135. FBIS
136. United Nations
137. World Tourism Organization (WTO)
138. FBIS
     U.S. News & World Report
139. U.S. Department of Agriculture
140. Amtorg Trading Company
     Pepsico
141. *The New York Times*
142. Visa International
143. Pepsico
144. *International Affairs*
145. *The New York Times*
146. *Pravda*
     The New York Times
147. *Moskovskiye Novosti*
     Strategic Review
148. *Moskovskiye Novosti*
     Strategic Review
149. Central Intelligence Agency (CIA)
     International Security
     Life
     Radio Liberty
150. *Newsweek*
151. U.S. Congress
152. *USA Today*

SOURCE

132. Same
133. U.S. Department of Transportation
134. *Statistical Abstract*
135. Same
136. *On An Average Day*
140. Department of Commerce
141. Motor Vehicle Manufacturers Association
    Statistical Abstract
142. Visa International
143. Pepsico
144. *The New York Times*
145. National Council on Alcoholism
146. *On An Average Day*
147. Same
148. U.S. Office of Management and Budget (OMB)
149. *On An Average Day*
    Department of Defense
150. *The New York Times*
152. Center for Defense Information

SOURCE

153. Gannett Press
     The New York Times
154. *Kommunist*
155. *Izvestia*
156. Radio Liberty
157. *Sovetskaya Rossia*
     Argumenty I Fakty
     Pravda
158. *U.S. News & World Report*
159. *Izvestia*
     United States Environmental Protection Agency (EPA)
     Worldwatch
160. Same
161. Dr. Murray Feshbach
162. *Moscow News*
     Soviet Life
163. *Maclean's*
     Moscow News
164. *Izvestia*
     Moscow News
165. Same
     National Public Radio (NPR)
166. *Izvestia*
167. *Soviet Life*
     Bulletin of the Atomic Scientist
168. *USA Today*
169. *Time*
170. CIA
     FBIS
171. *Izvestia*

236

SOURCE

153. Gannett Papers
    The New York Times
154. Natural Resources Defense Council
155. *Science*
156. *New York Times*
    National Network to Prevent Birth Defects
157. Natural Resources Defense Council
    The New York Times
    USA Today
158. EPA
159. EPA
    Worldwatch Institute
    USA Today
    Statistical Abstract
160. *Science News*
161. *USA Today*
    The New York Times
162. Bureau of Labor Statistics
    USA Today
163. National Council on Alcoholism Inc.
164. National Safety Council
165. U.S. Department of Labor

SOURCE

172. FBIS
173. Same
174. Radio Liberty
175. *Izvestia*
    World Press Review
    Ward's Auto World
176. *Science*
    Business Week
177. U.S. Congress
    The New York Times
178. FBIS
179. *Business Week*
180. *The New York Times*
    U.S. Department of Agriculture
181. *USA Today*
182. *Business Week*
    U.S. News & World Report
183. FBIS
    Moscow News
184. *World Press Review*
185. *Izvestia*
186. Same
187. Same
188. Same
189. FBIS
    Argumenty I Fakty
190. FBIS
    Radio Liberty
191. *Moscow News*
    FBIS

SOURCE

172. Consumer Product Safety Commission
     National Safety Council
173. *Statistical Abstract*
174. Electronic Industries Association
     A.C. Nielsen
175. *Statistical Abstract*
176. Same
177. Same
179. *Business Week*
180. Author's research
181. Same
182. U.S. Congressional Hearings
183. Department of Commerce
     The New York Times
     USA Today
184. *Forbes*
185. Bureau of Justice Statistics
186. Same
187. Same
188. Same
189. *On An Average Day*
190. FBI
191. Insurance Information Institute

SOURCE

192. *Pravda*
    FBIS
    Radio Liberty
193. *Izvestia*
    Pravda
194. Radio Liberty
195. USSR
196. FBIS
197. Same
198. *Pravda*
    Newsweek
199. Radio Liberty
    Pravda International
200. FBIS
    Radio Liberty
201. Radio Liberty
    FBIS
202. Radio Liberty
203. *Izvestia*
204. Soviet Union
    Izvestia
205. *The New York Times*
    Soviet Union
206. *Argumenty I Fakty*
    Radio Liberty
207. Radio Liberty
208. *Izvestia*
209. *People's Economy*
    Dr. Murray Feshbach
210. Radio Liberty
211. *Moscow News*

192. National Safety Council
On An Average Day
193. National Safety Council
194. *Newsweek*
Handgun Control
U.S. News & World Report
195. *U.S. News & World Report*
196. FBI
197. Same
198. *Business Week*
FBI
199. Bureau of Justice Statistics
200. Same
201. Same
202. National Coalition for the Homeless
203. *Wall Street Journal*
Bureau of the Census
204. Same
205. Same
206. *Statistical Abstract*
207. U.S. Department of Labor
208. *Statistical Abstract*
209. National Gay & Lesbian Task Force
210. *Yearbook of American and Canadian Churches*
211. Same

SOURCE

SOURCE

213. National Center for Health Statistics
     The Official Catholic Directory
214. Center for Book Research, University of Scranton
215. CBS News
216. *Statistical Abstract*
217. U.S. Department of Agriculture
218. Circus Education Specialists, Inc.
     Time
219. Recording Industry Association of America (RIAA)
220. U.S. Information Security Oversight Office